Philippe Legendre

KIDS CAN DRAW
Animals

KIDS CAN DRAW
Animals

Walter Foster

Contents

Forest Animals

Favorite Pets

Farm Animals

Donkey	55
Cow	57
Pig	59
Goat	61
Sheep	63
Chicken	65
Horse	67
Goose	69
Rooster	71

Dinosaurs

Iguanodon	77
Dimetrodon	79
Diplodocus	81
Triceratops	83
Pteranodon	85
Tyrannosaurus Rex	87
Stegosaurus	89
Pterodactyl	91
Ankylosaurus	93

Attention Parents and Teachers

All children can draw a circle, a square, or a triangle . . . which means that they can also learn to draw a bear, a dog, a cow, or a hedgehog! The KIDS CAN DRAW learning method is easy and fun. Children will learn a technique and a vocabulary of shapes that will form the basis for all kinds of drawing.

Pictures are created by combining geometric shapes to form a mass of volumes and surfaces. From this stage, children can give character to their sketches with straight, curved, or broken lines.

With just a few strokes of the pencil, an animal will appear—and with the addition of color, the picture will be a true work of art!

The KIDS CAN DRAW method offers a real apprenticeship in technique and a first look at composition, proportion, shapes, and lines. The simplicity of this method ensures that the pleasure of drawing is always the most important factor.

About Philippe Legendre

French painter, engraver, and illustrator, Philippe Legendre also runs a school of art for children aged 6–14 years. Legendre frequently spends time in schools and has developed this method of learning so that all children can discover the artist within themselves.

Helpful Tips

1. Every picture is made up of simple geometric shapes, which are illustrated at the top of each left-hand page. This is called the **Vocabulary of Shapes.** Encourage children to practice drawing each shape before starting their pictures.

2. Suggest that children use a pencil to do their sketches. This way, if they don't like a particular shape, they can just erase it and try again.

3. A dotted line indicates that the line should be erased. Have children draw the whole shape and then erase the dotted part of the line.

4. Once children finish their drawings, they can color them with crayons, colored pencils, or felt-tip markers. They may want to go over the lines with a black pencil or pen.

Now let's get started!

KIDS CAN DRAW
Forest Animals

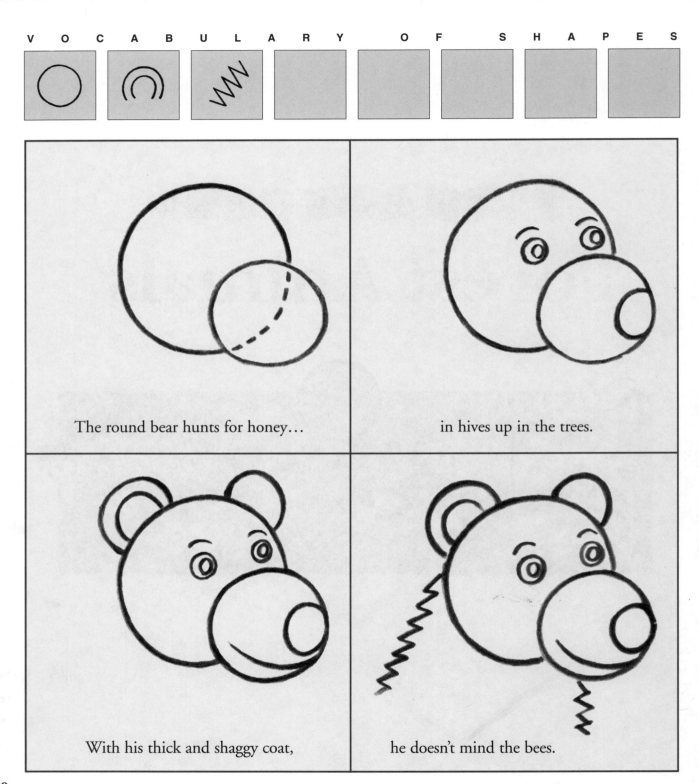

The round bear hunts for honey…

in hives up in the trees.

With his thick and shaggy coat,

he doesn't mind the bees.

Bear

With an oval body...

and a pointy nose,

the spiky little hedgehog...

wears pins instead of clothes!

Hedgehog

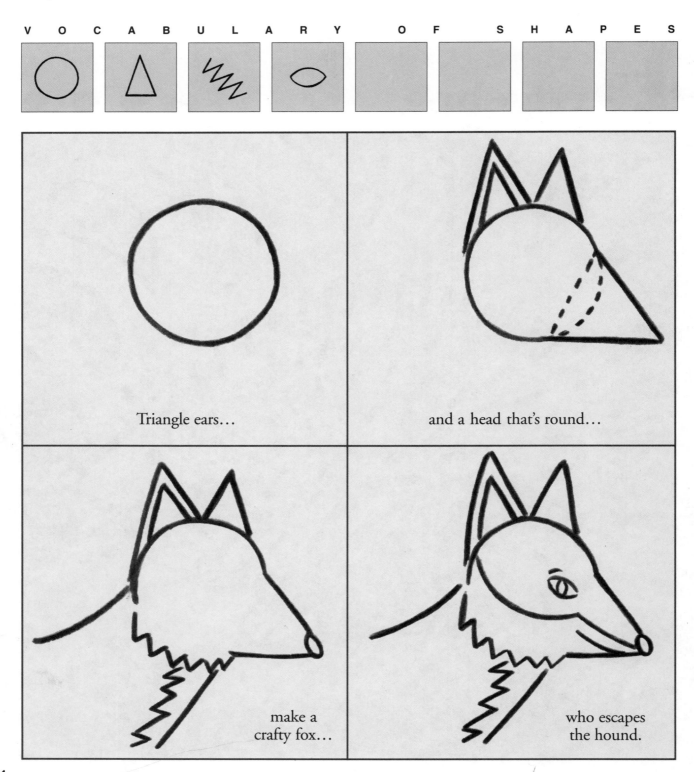

Triangle ears…

and a head that's round…

make a
crafty fox…

who escapes
the hound.

14

Fox

The long-necked deer...

hides among the trees.

When there's a noise,

she quickly flees.

16

Deer

Make three round balls...

and a tail with a curl.

Next thing you know,

you've made a squirrel!

18

Squirrel

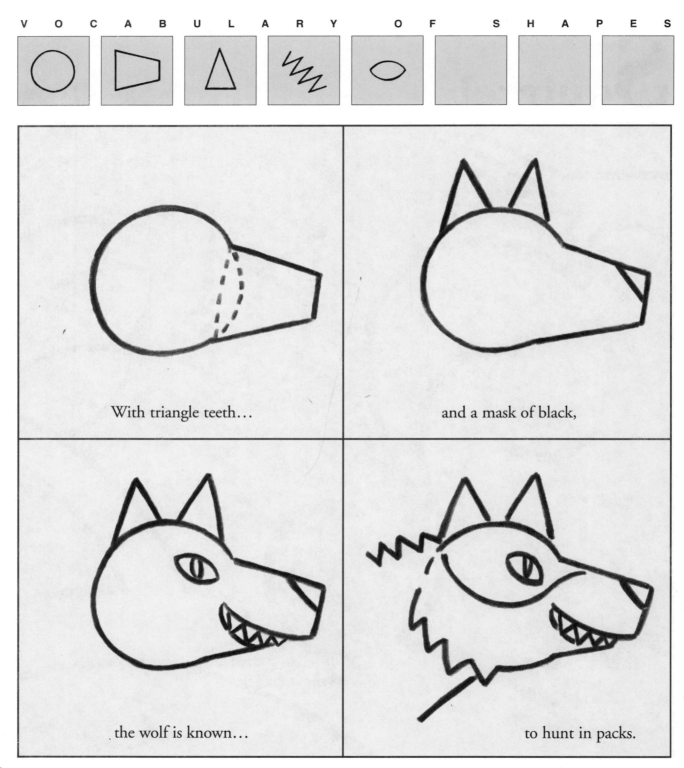

With triangle teeth…

and a mask of black,

the wolf is known…

to hunt in packs.

20

Wolf

With circles on her coat and face,

the lynx looks like a cat...

from outer space!

22

Lynx

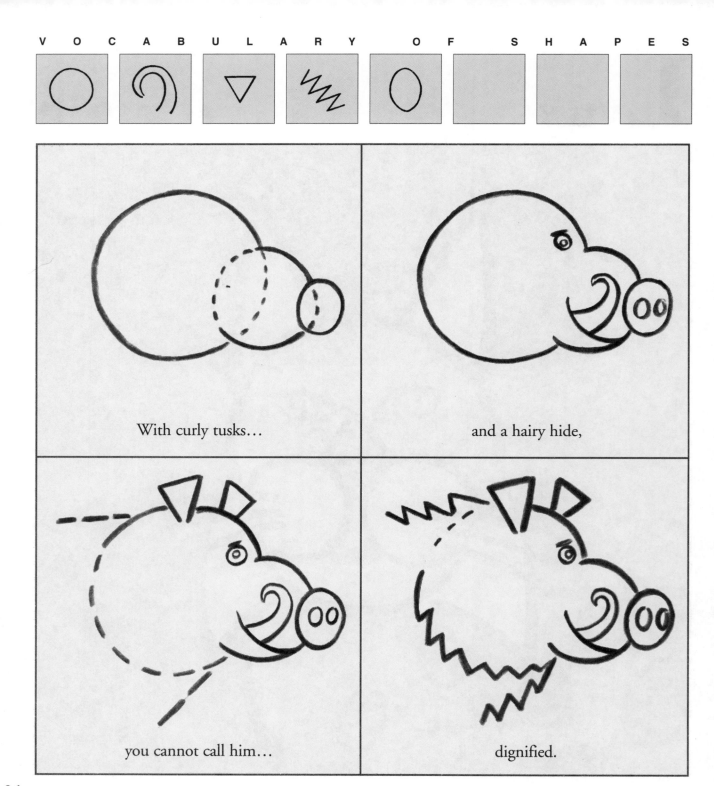

With curly tusks...

and a hairy hide,

you cannot call him...

dignified.

24

Wild **B**oar

They say the owl...

is very wise...

with triangle feathers...

and circle eyes.

O_{wl}

In the forest you have drawn, the animals are on the prowl.

You can make the wise owl hoot and the fierce wolf growl.

KIDS CAN DRAW

Favorite Pets

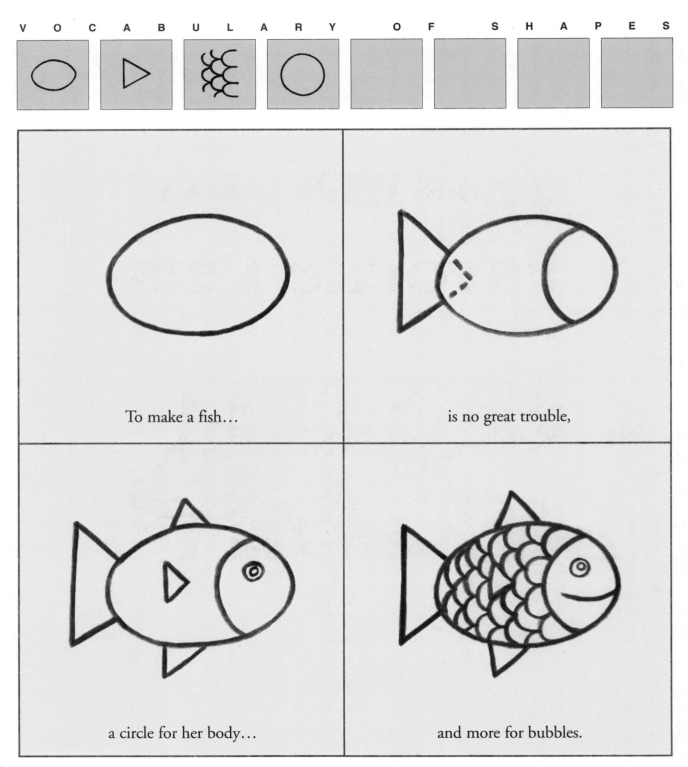

To make a fish…

is no great trouble,

a circle for her body…

and more for bubbles.

Fish

If you draw…

some curly doodles,

soon you'll see…

a fluffy poodle.

34

Poodle

A circle makes…

the head atop…

a bunny that…

goes hippity-hop.

36

Bunny

You can almost hear the cat purr,

when you draw stripes...

on her fur.

38

Cat

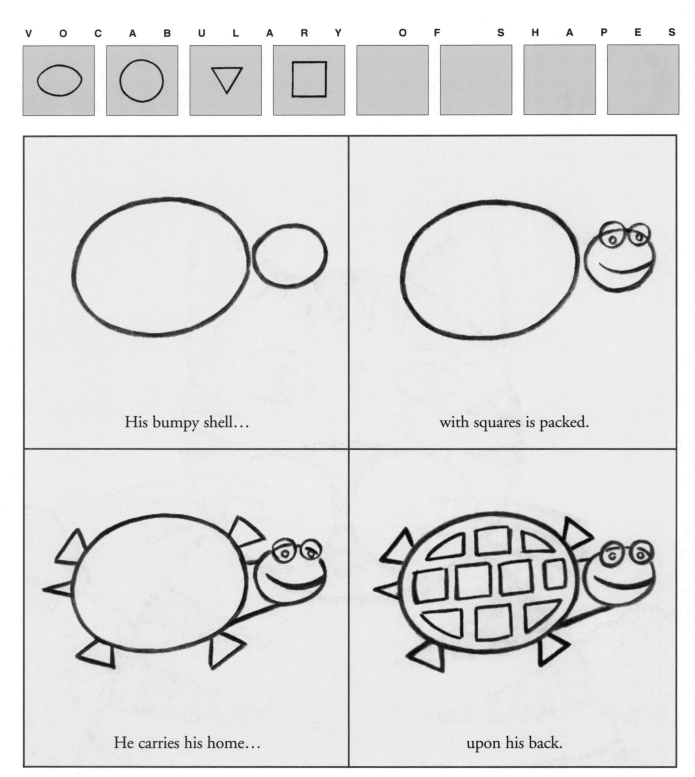

His bumpy shell…

with squares is packed.

He carries his home…

upon his back.

Turtle

The mouse has…

rounded ears like these.

It makes her smile…

to think of cheese.

42

Mouse

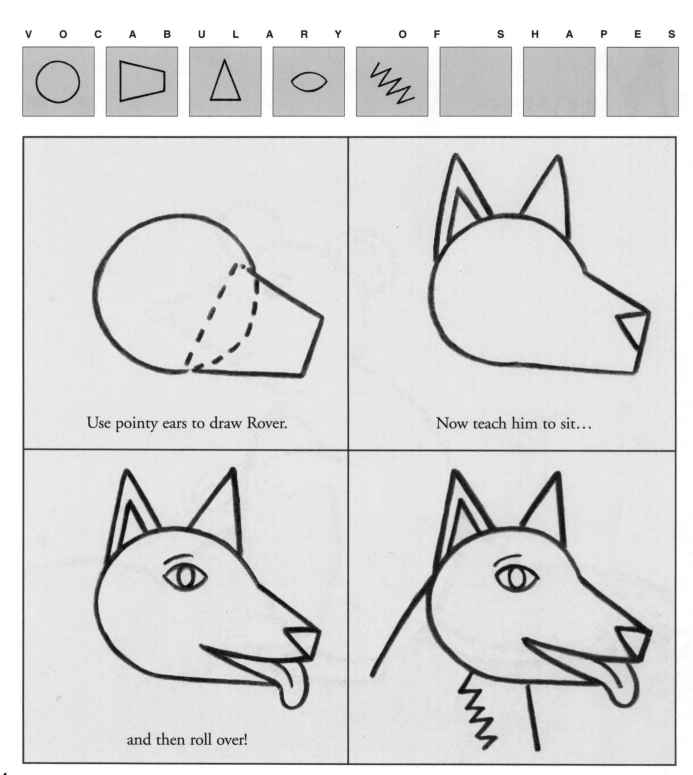

Use pointy ears to draw Rover.

Now teach him to sit...

and then roll over!

Dog

To draw this furry fellow,

make a half-circle big.

But don't draw a curly tail—

he's not a real pig!

Guinea Pig

This brightly colored bird...

has triangles for feet.

"Polly wants a cracker,"

says the parakeet.

48

Parakeet

At last, you can draw your favorite pets—from a trusty dog to a little mouse.

Now make a pretty picture of them living in your house.

KIDS CAN DRAW
Farm Animals

Here's the round donkey in gray.

He starts each morning…

with a loud bray.

Donkey

Make a square nose...

so the cow can chew.

She can make some milk for you.

Cow

The happy pig...

is very round.

He must weigh...

a lot of pounds.

P_{ig}

Diamonds make ears…

for a gentle goat.

A beard grows upon his throat.

Goat

Half-circles make the sheep...

look right. Her fleece is...

like a cloud of white.

Sheep

The chicken's feet are...

made of sticks.

Behind her follow little chicks.

Chicken

65

A blocky head helps the horse eat hay...

so he can gallop far away.

Horse

With a triangle beak,

she honks and roams…

around her barnyard home.

68

Goose

The round rooster…

that you drew…

now sings
cock-a-doodle-doo!

70

Rooster

Milking cows and feeding pigs are common farmyard chores.

But if you've drawn a farm of animals, you've done the task that's yours.

KIDS CAN DRAW

Dinosaurs

The iguanodon…

has big square teeth,

but don't be scared—

she just eats leaves.

76

Iguanodon

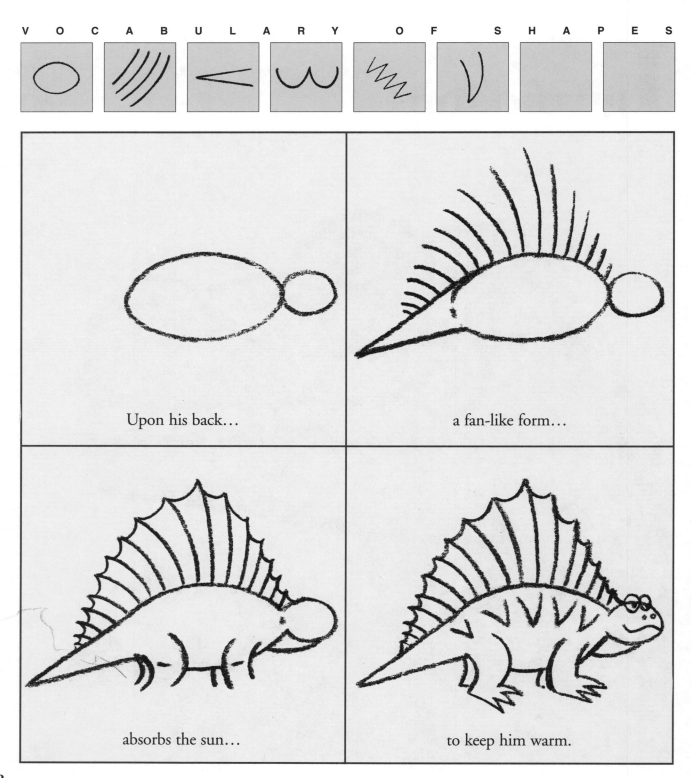

Upon his back…

a fan-like form…

absorbs the sun…

to keep him warm.

Dimetrodon

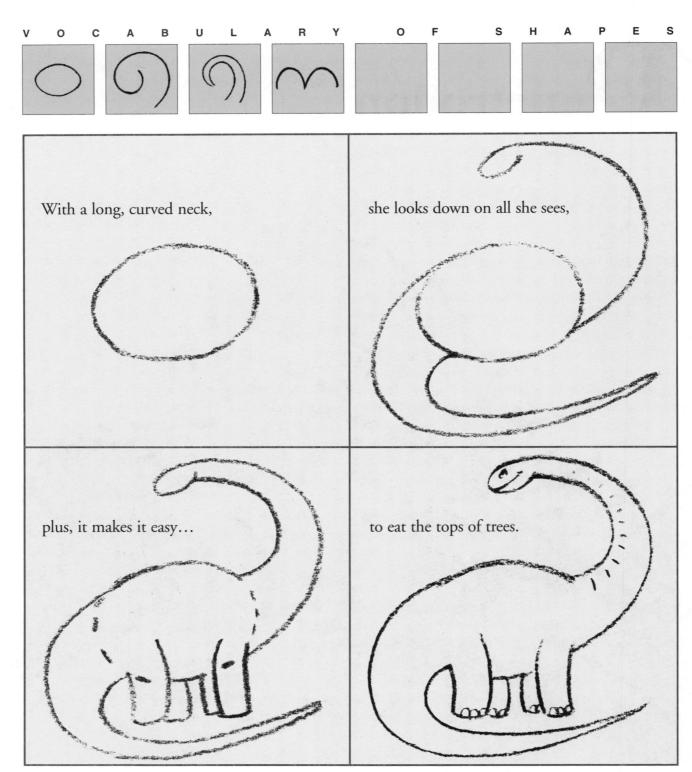

With a long, curved neck,

she looks down on all she sees,

plus, it makes it easy…

to eat the tops of trees.

Diplodocus

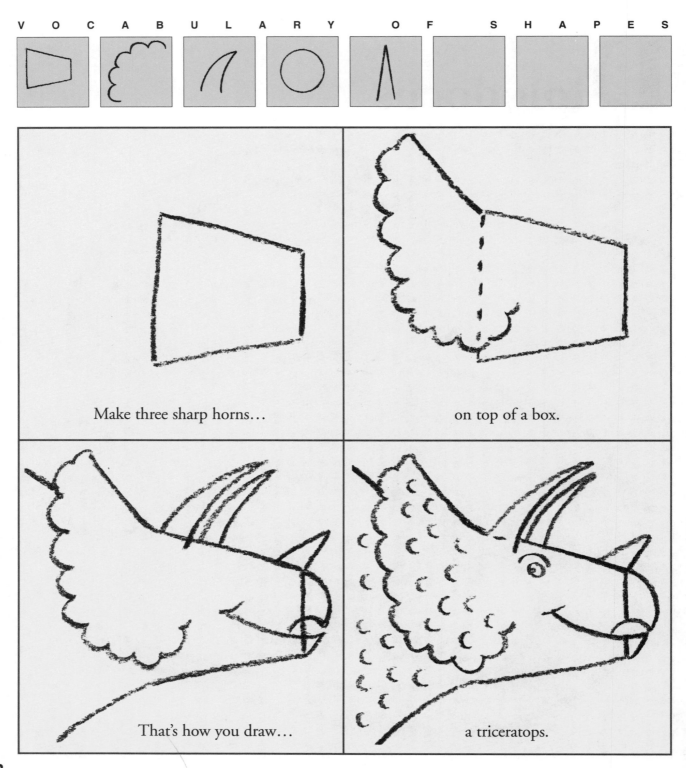

Make three sharp horns…

on top of a box.

That's how you draw…

a triceratops.

82

Triceratops

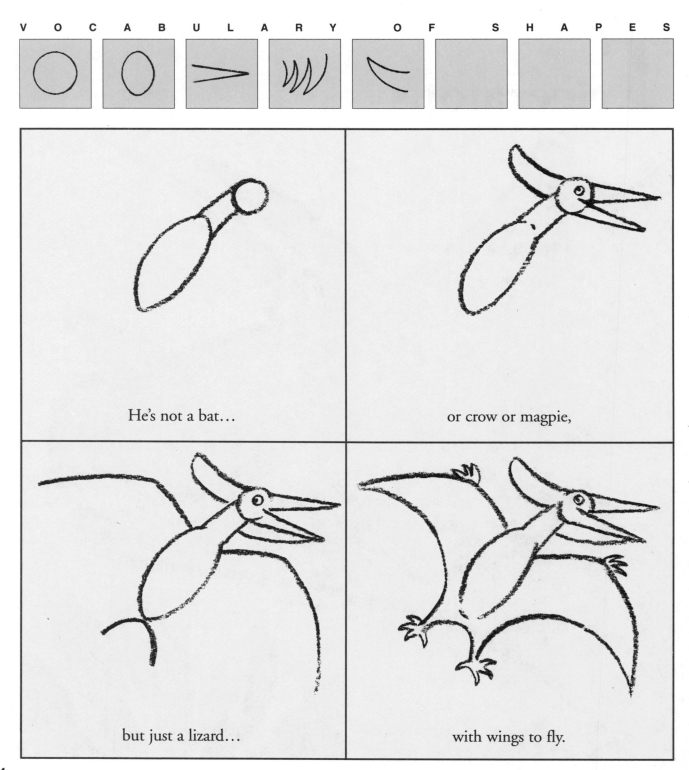

He's not a bat...

or crow or magpie,

but just a lizard...

with wings to fly.

Pteranodon

With his square jaw,

this beastly king…

can catch and eat…

most anything.

86

Tyrannosaurus **R**ex

On his back...

is a diamond wall,

but his brain...

is very small.

Stegosaurus

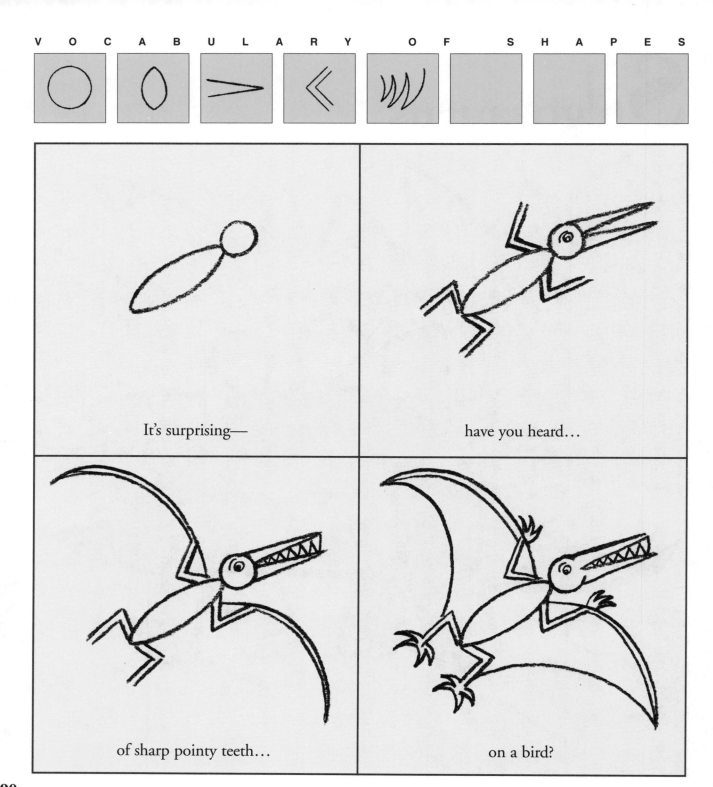

Pterodactyl

With triangles covering…

her back and flank,

She looks just like…

an armored tank.

Ankylosaurus

Even though the dinosaurs are extinct,

Ankylosaurus

Even though the dinosaurs are extinct,

you can recreate each one with colored inks.

Walter Foster™

Walter Foster Publishing, Inc.
23062 La Cadena Drive
Laguna Hills, CA 92653 USA
www.walterfoster.com
ISBN 1-56010-444-9
UPC 0-50283-33320-3

Forest Animals, original title *J'apprends à dessiner les animaux de la forêt*, © 1992;
Favorite Pets, original title *J'apprends à dessiner les animaux de la maison*, © 1992; Farm
Animals, original title *J'apprends à dessiner les animaux de la ferme*, © 1992; Dinosaurs,
original title *J'apprends à dessiner les dinosaures*, © 1994, Editions Fleurus, Paris.